A
DESERT
YEAR

A DESERT YEAR

CAROL LERNER

MORROW JUNIOR BOOKS / NEW YORK

For Kitty. The best.

The author thanks Dr. Richard Zweifel and Frances Zweifel of Portal, Arizona, for reviewing the text.

Watercolors were used for the full-color art.
The text type is 12 point Janson.

Printed in Singapore at Tien Wah Press.
1 2 3 4 5 6 7 8 9 10
Library of Congress Cataloging-in-Publication Data
Lerner, Carol.
A desert year / Carol Lerner.
p. cm.
Includes bibliographical references.
Summary: A study of the animals and plants found in the desert of
America's southwest.
ISBN 0-688-09382-5 (trade).—ISBN 0-688-09383-3 (library)
1. Desert ecology—Southwestern States—Juvenile literature.
2. Desert fauna—Southwestern States—Juvenile literature.
3. Desert flora—Southwestern States—Juvenile literature.
[1. Desert ecology—Southwestern States. 2. Desert animals—
Southwestern States. 3. Desert plants—Southwestern States.]
I. Title.
QH104.5.S6L47 1991
574.5'2652'0979—dc20 90-44643 CIP AC

The North American desert stretches from southern Oregon and Idaho, in the north, far down into Mexico. In the United States, it lies between two great mountain chains—the Rocky Mountains on the east and the Sierra Nevada and Cascade Mountains on the west. Over this great distance, there are many differences in landscape, in soils, and in weather and temperatures. Great stretches are nearly barren, while others hold a rich variety of plant life. But some conditions are the same throughout this vast space: dryness and great swings in daily temperatures. Water is almost always in short supply in deserts, and the change of temperature from day to night may be as much as 80° F.

This book looks at some of the plants and animals in the hot deserts of the southwestern United States to see how they live through the year in this harsh world.

Winter days are often sunny and mild and may reach a comfortable 70° F., but nights are cool and temperatures sometimes drop below freezing. Food is scarce now, but the desert animals have found ways of living through this season. Just as in colder climates, some mammals hibernate in protected places. Although some areas are without trees or other large plants that can provide shelter, the desert earth offers a safe home to many kinds of animals. The hibernators enter a deep sleep, their bodies cool, and their heartbeats and breathing slow down. In this state, they use up very little energy and can live for months on their body fat. Other mammals simply stay in warm burrows and rest there for days or weeks at a time until hunger drives them into activity. But most large mammals have no snug underground homes. In winter, even the animals that are usually active at night are likely to be out looking for food in the warmer daylight hours.

Some desert rodents that live on seeds have fur-lined pockets on each side of their mouths that they use for carrying food. The LITTLE POCKET MOUSE is named for these cheek pouches. This animal stays underground for months. In hibernation, its body cools until its temperature is about the same as the burrow's. Its breathing becomes uneven—sometimes stopping entirely for as long as five minutes. After a few days or a week, it may wake and eat a few of its stored seeds before going back into another period of hibernation.

The WESTERN SPOTTED SKUNK is the smallest skunk in the United States; it is the size of a half-grown house cat. It does not hibernate but, during periods of cool weather, spends more time napping and resting in its underground den. It leaves the burrow to hunt for mice and other small animals.

BADGERS also live in grasslands and in some forests, but they are well suited to desert life. With long claws and strong, flattened bodies, they are powerful earth movers. They throw up great piles of dirt when they dig their underground homes or search for small rodents living in tunnels in the earth. Badgers do not hibernate.

The PECCARY, or JAVELINA (hahv-uh-LEE-nuh), is a wild pig found in parts of Arizona, New Mexico, and Texas. It travels in groups and is active at all seasons. It eats cacti, seeds, and roots and other underground plant parts. In summer, the peccary searches for food when the sun is low; but in winter, it may be active in the warmest part of the day to take advantage of the heat.

WINTER—BIRDS

The summer birds—those that come to the hot desert each year only to mate and raise their young—have been gone for months. But many birds stay in the desert all through the year, and others come just for the winter. The winter visitors are birds that prefer to nest in cooler places. Last summer they were in the north or high up in nearby mountains. Many of them are seed eaters that feed on the ground, searching the desert floor for food. Here no deep or long-lasting snows hide the fallen seeds from sight.

The ROADRUNNER's body becomes chilled on winter nights. After sunrise it goes to an open space, spreads its wings, and raises its feathers so the sun's rays can reach the patches of black skin on its back. Black absorbs heat faster than any other color. When its temperature rises, the roadrunner goes hunting for its food. Because there are fewer insects in winter and most of the reptiles are in hibernation, it may be forced to eat some plant food during this season.

Some of the year-round birds have habits that protect them from cold winter nights as well as from the heat of summer. CACTUS WRENS make their nests in cactus plants or in trees or bushes and use them throughout the year—not just when raising their young. Every adult cactus wren, male as well as female, has its own winter roosting nest and uses it at night. These birds live on insects and other small animal prey.

Night-flying insects, caught in midair, are the POORWILL's main food. When the weather cools and these insects become scarce, some poorwills hibernate. No other bird is known to do this. Hibernating poorwills have been found on rocky cliffs and inside the trunks of dead cactus plants.

CHESTNUT-COLLARED LONGSPURS (the *longspur* is the long back toe and claw on its feet) nest in northern states and in Canada but move to southwestern deserts for winter. Plant seeds make up their entire winter diet. In this season, both the male and female are drab-looking birds. When spring comes, the male's appearance will change dramatically. New feathers of yellow, chestnut, and black will grow in to replace its dull winter covering.

*male chestnut-
collared longspur
in spring*

WINTER—REPTILES AND AMPHIBIANS

Amphibians are usually animals of wet habitats. They are present in deserts only at places and times that water is available— where springs flow from the ground or when summer rains soak the earth and leave pools. Reptiles—and especially lizards—are almost everywhere. Reptiles lose water through their skins less easily than mammals do. The scales on reptile bodies hold the moisture inside, and some reptile skins are nearly waterproof. Unlike mammals and birds, reptiles and amphibians cannot produce enough heat to keep them warm. They usually escape from winter by hibernating underground or in deep cracks among the rocks. They stay there through the cold months, lying numb and quiet. But because winters in these southern deserts are mild, a few species are above ground even in this season.

The GILA (HE-luh) MONSTER has spots of black and orange (or yellow or pink), and its back is covered with round, beadlike scales. It is the largest lizard in the United States (usually eighteen to twenty-four inches long). The gila

monster and its close relative, the Mexican beaded lizard, are the only poisonous lizards. The gila monster hibernates in winter, living on the fat stored in its plump tail. When it comes out of hibernation in spring, the tail may be only one-fifth of its previous size. It will fatten up again as the animal starts feeding on birds' eggs and small rodents.

DESERT IGUANAS (ih-GWAHN-uhs) are big animals that grow to a length of sixteen inches. These are heat-loving lizards. They go into hibernation early in fall and are the last lizards to become active in spring.

The WESTERN DIAMONDBACK RATTLESNAKE is one of ten kinds of rattlesnakes found in North American deserts. It is the largest snake in the western United States, growing to six or seven feet long. The diamondback hibernates, but in the southern deserts it may awaken during warm spells and take a sunbath for a few hours.

The SIDE-BLOTCHED LIZARD, too, often wakes from its deep sleep and comes out on warm, sunny days. First it sits in the sun to warm itself. As its body absorbs heat, the lizard changes color. The male is dark all over when its body is cool; as it heats up, the spots begin to show. Once warm, the lizard starts looking for insects.

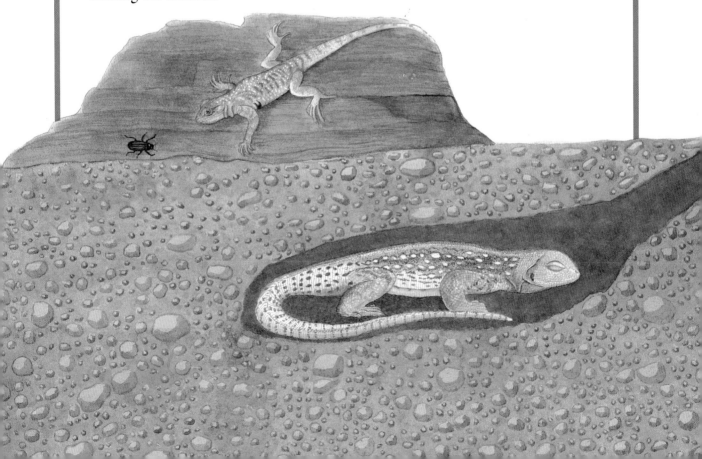

Like reptiles and amphibians, arthropod animals are unable to move when their surroundings are too cool. In very cold temperatures they may freeze to death. Some winged insects do as birds do and fly to warmer places before winter comes. Among those that stay, the adults of many species die at the end of the growing season, leaving behind eggs or immature offspring that will survive the winter and change to adults next year. Arthropods that live as adults from year to year take shelter from the cold, and most enter a resting state in the coldest months of winter. In this condition, they can endure lower temperatures without harm. Some species that live in these warm deserts spring into activity on sunny winter days.

Adult MESQUITE (meh-SKEET) TWIG GIRDLERS live for only a few weeks in the late fall. They feed on the tender bark of mesquite and other trees, making a cut that circles, or girdles, a branch and kills it. Females lay their eggs in this dead wood. The eggs soon hatch, and the young larvae, or caterpillars, feed on the wood and remain there for the next eight or nine months.

During the coldest months, DARKLING BEETLE adults remain inactive in underground burrows. These insects are sometimes called stink beetles or circus beetles. When they are threatened, they do a headstand and spray the enemy with a bad-smelling liquid that comes out from the rear of their bodies.

About twenty different species of tarantulas are found in the Southwest. Female tarantulas may live for a long time—some have survived for thirty years. Like other tarantulas, the DESERT TARANTULA spends most of its time in a burrow. When cold weather comes, it plugs up the opening and waits for the return of warm weather. These spiders use poison to kill their insect prey, but the poison is not strong enough to injure a person seriously.

HARVESTER ANTS live on the seeds of wildflowers, grasses, and other plants. The colony digs a complicated tunnel system in the ground—sometimes ten to fifteen feet deep. In these deep tunnels, the ants are safe from both cold and heat. They bring seeds into the tunnels and store them in grain rooms. The seed supply provides food during the seasons when the desert offers little to eat. On warm days, the ants may come up during the time around noon to search for food.

mesquite
twig girdler
and girdled
branch

darkling beetle
in headstand

Shrubs are the commonest plants in deserts. Shrubs, like cacti, are perennials—plants that live for several or many years. In the desert they often look as if they had been planted in a pattern, with wide, even spaces between each of them. But this space is not really empty. It is filled with a network of shallow roots coming from each bush. In a land with little rainfall, many plants spread their roots over a large area so they can collect enough water to stay alive. Beneath some of the shrubs, seeds are just taking root, even in this season. These plants are called winter annuals. Their seeds sprout after winter rains if the temperatures are neither too cold nor too warm. Because the days are cool, they grow slowly. In spring they flower, make their seeds, and then die.

BRITTLEBUSH is a common desert shrub that blooms between November and May. Its yellow flowers are on long bare stems that rise above the leafy branches. The plant produces two sets of leaves and flowers each year—after the summer rains and again after the winter rains. Its leaves are covered with a thick mat of short hairs, giving them a gray-green appearance. Many desert plants have this kind of fuzzy surface. The hairs form a loose blanket over the leaf. They act as an insulating layer against the heat and cold and may also reduce the amount of water lost into the dry air.

WHITE BUR SAGE, another common shrub, is sometimes called burrobush because donkeys like to eat it. This plant is bare now. In spring it will have leaves covered by short hairs, like the leaves of brittlebush. Bur sage sends up many new shoots from its underground stems, and in time there is a little forest of dead and living branches growing up from a single shrub. It acts as a "nurse plant" for desert annuals, because wind-blown soil and bits of dead plant materials are caught by the branches and pile up at the bottom of the shrub. The litter provides a good seedbed for the annuals.

Winter annuals will not sprout in warm temperatures. The seeds may remain in the ground for years until their growth is triggered by just the right combination of moisture and cool temperatures. The green leaves of the annuals, such as this PHACELIA (fuh-SEE-lee-uh), help to nourish the desert rodents that are searching for winter food.

brittlebush
leaf

white bur sage
leaf (enlarged)

phacelia
flowers

Spring temperatures often reach the 80s or higher. With warmer and longer days, hibernators awake from their deep sleep and the other animals become more active. Some parts of the desert receive a large part of the year's scanty rainfall in the winter months. If those rains have been poor, there will be less new plant growth. With less food, the small mammals may delay their mating, and their litters will have fewer young. But if the rains have been plentiful and the desert plants flourish, the animals find good supplies of plant and insect food. With this rich diet their bodies are soon ready to mate and have young. A population explosion among the plant-eating animals promises plenty of food for the meat eaters, too.

Except for its long tail, the ROUND-TAILED GROUND SQUIRREL looks like a little prairie dog. Like other ground squirrels, it makes its home in an underground burrow. These squirrels mate between February and April, and as many as twelve young are born about a month afterward. The number is closely tied to the amount of rain that fell the previous autumn and winter. Heavier rains bring greater amounts of nourishing plant food for the mother, and each extra inch of rain can mean one more baby in the litter.

The mating of BLACK-TAILED JACKRABBITS is not closely tied to the seasons. They may mate almost year-round, although there is a peak in breeding after winter rains. Jackrabbits are really hares. Unlike rabbits, jackrabbits are born with a full coat of fur and with eyes wide open, and are able to stand alone and take a few steps.

At least twenty-seven kinds of bats are found in North American deserts, and many are important plant pollinators, spreading pollen from flower to flower as they feed. SANBORN'S LONG-NOSED BAT spends the winter in Mexico and returns to the United States desert in May. Adults fly after sundown to feed on insects and on the nectar and pollen of flowers.

The KIT FOX has big ears and dainty legs. It is the smallest North American fox; it weighs up to four or five pounds and is about the size of a large house cat. As with other foxes, male and female share in feeding the young. Kit fox babies are born in February or March and live on their mother's milk for the first ten weeks. Then they are ready for meat. This kit fox is hunting for rats, mice, and ground squirrels to feed its pups.

Sanborn's
long-nosed
bat

Spring means the beginning of the nesting season, and in the desert spring comes as early as February. Daytime temperatures are already high. Flowering begins in March, and with the flowers come armies of insects that can be fed to nestling birds. The year-round birds are usually the first to lay their eggs. These pairs may have been together in the same spot all winter. Birds returning from the south must find a mate and claim a territory before they are ready to start a family.

CURVE-BILLED THRASHERS live in the desert all year. Thrashers begin nesting as early as March and may continue into August. A pair might raise three sets of babies in a year. Thrashers most often build their nests in cholla (CHOY-yuh) cactus plants. The cactus spines protect the nest from snakes and other enemies, but sometimes a baby thrasher is killed on the needles as it leaves the nest.

GILA (HE-luh) WOODPECKERS are also year-round desert birds. Male and female work together to peck out a deep nest in a giant cactus or in a cottonwood or willow tree. Here the eggs and young will be safe from heat and the drying wind. On a hot day, a nest inside a living cactus will be 20° to 25° F. cooler than the air outside.

The GAMBEL'S QUAIL, another all-year bird, lives most of the year in a flock of twenty to one hundred quails. Nesting depends on the amount of rain that falls in late winter. After a good rainfall there is plenty of plant food. The flock breaks up as the well-fed birds go off to find a mate. If plant growth is poor, the birds stay in the flock and wait until the next year to mate.

Many WHITE-WINGED DOVES spend the winter in Mexico and return to southern parts of California, Arizona, New Mexico, and Texas in April and May. Like other doves, they make a simple, flat nest in a tree or a large cactus plant. Since the nest provides no shade or protection from the sun, the eggs could easily become overheated. The adults cover the eggs with their own bodies to keep them cool, and one of the parents is always on the nest. Male doves have a lower body temperature than do the females. Males sit on the eggs during the hottest parts of the day.

The bright spring sunshine soaks through layers of earth. As the warmth spreads down, the cold-blooded hibernators stir, crawl from their holes, and bask in the sun to warm themselves. In a few weeks, heat and dryness will drive these animals back to shelter during the hottest daylight hours. But now the sun's warmth is welcome. After months without eating, the first need is food. But soon most reptiles will start searching for a mate. For amphibians, desert life seems almost impossible. Amphibians lose water through their skins at a rate that is one hundred times faster than that of some desert reptiles. In addition, their eggs and newly hatched young need to be in water. In spite of these difficulties, some species of toads are true desert animals and live here successfully.

As long as there are juicy plants to eat, the DESERT TORTOISE gets plenty of water from its food and stores some (about one cup) in its huge bladder. It will use this water later, when the plants have become dry. Pairs begin to mate soon after they emerge from hibernation. Females bury the eggs and leave them to hatch on their own. Turtle eggs, like bird eggs, have hard shells that protect the young within and keep them from drying out. The earth around the buried eggs prevents them from overheating.

The COACHWHIP is one of several kinds of whip snakes in western deserts. Whip snakes are slender and fast-moving. Unlike most desert snakes, they are active in daytime—climbing trees and bushes to find nestling birds and entering burrows to capture small rodents. Whip snakes mate in spring, and the female lays her eggs a few weeks later. Like most egg-laying snakes, she deserts the eggs after laying them.

After mating, female horned lizards dig a tunnel, lay their eggs inside, and fill it up again. Horned lizards are named for the spiny horns on their heads. When they are above ground, they blend into the background and are well hidden from enemies. In addition, the TEXAS HORNED LIZARD has a last-ditch defense when it is cornered: It squirts a thin stream of blood from its eyelids. Some chemical in the blood seems to irritate other animals, and predators such as foxes are repelled by it.

RED-SPOTTED TOADS usually live near a spring or some other place with permanent water. They come out to mate after rainfall, anytime from April to September. In dry periods, these small, flat toads hide in cracks among the rocks or underground.

At this season of new life and growth, the desert stirs with the activities of hungry animals, large and small. Plant-eating arthropods are feeding eagerly on the spring plants, and meat eaters are just as busy hunting prey. Like other desert animals, arthropods move constantly in and out of shelter as the air and ground get warmer or cooler. But the arthropods have one great advantage over larger animals. Being little, they fit into tiny spaces. Within the vast burning desert, they find crannies just big enough to hold them. Many take refuge underground.

Caterpillars of the WHITE-LINED SPHINX MOTH hatch from their eggs and begin to feed on the spring wildflowers. Soft-bodied caterpillars are in danger of overheating and losing moisture in hot, dry air. When the sun is high, most caterpillars are on their plants, shaded by the leaves and stems. By the time summer comes, with its intense heat that dries up the food plants, they will have changed into moths and flown away.

Many kinds of bees are visiting the flowers and spreading pollen as they feed. This female DIGGER BEE has made a hole. She will stock it with pollen and nectar and lay her egg in the tunnel. After the young bee hatches, it will feed and grow in the safety of the tunnel. Next spring, it will change to an adult and dig its way out of the soil.

About twenty different kinds of SCORPIONS live in these deserts. They come out to hunt at night, killing their prey—insects and other scorpions—by stinging them with a poisonous barb on the end of the "tail." The poison of one species is so strong it can kill a human being. This female mated last summer, but her young will not be born until July or August. They will be born alive and active and will immediately climb up on their mother's back. They will stay there until they are ready to shed their skins for the first time, and then they will scatter.

A troop of FUNGUS-GROWING ANTS comes out from its underground tunnels to collect leaves and bits of flowers. These ants carry this plant material back inside and chew it into a fine pulp. Molds will grow on the pile of plant litter, aided by moist air that is trapped in the chamber beneath the dry desert. This mold is the only food the ant colony eats.

white-lined sphinx moth
adult

SPRING—PLANTS

After a winter with good rainfall, the desert puts on a dazzling flower show. When weather conditions were exactly right for one of the desert annuals, that species flowers in huge numbers in the spring. But the different species have different requirements for rainfall and temperature, so perhaps only two or three kinds of flowers may dominate the year's display. Desert annuals are called ephemerals because they live for such a short time. Their stems, leaves, and roots have no special adaptations for desert life. They survive here because they complete their life cycle quickly, escaping the heat and dryness of the summer. In a few weeks they will be dead, leaving only their seeds behind. The next generation will not appear in large numbers until the right weather conditions occur again—possibly not for three or five years or more. Perennial plants are blooming now, too. These include trees and shrubs, cacti, and some wildflowers that come up each year from long-lived underground parts.

MEXICAN GOLD POPPY is a widespread desert annual, a close relative of the California poppy. As many as thirty-five flowers may grow from a single plant. Masses of poppies appear in some springs, covering great patches of earth with gold. PURPLE OWL CLOVER, another annual, often flowers along with the poppies.

The flame-red DESERT MARIPOSA (mar-uh-POH-suh) is a perennial. Like many other members of the lily family, it grows from an underground bulb that lives from year to year. It may appear as a single plant or as part of a large colony.

Because of the shape of its flat stems, this cactus is called BEAVER-TAIL. It grows in a low clump, its pads covered with clusters of tiny hooked hairs rather than long spines. Its bright purple flowers are followed by pear-shaped fruits. Another name for the plant is prickly pear, because the fruits are covered by the same barbed hairs. The little hairs sting and are almost impossible to get out of either skin or clothing.

SUMMER—MAMMALS

It is morning on a cloudless summer day. The night was cool, but now the earth is baking in the heat of the sun. By afternoon, air temperatures may reach 110° F., and a thermometer on the surface of the soil will show 150° F. At these temperatures, activity is impossible for most mammals, and they may become so hot that their lives are in danger. Some can cool off by sweating or panting, but this means losing water from the body, and the desert offers few opportunities to drink. Most escape the heat by hiding from the sun in the daytime. They find shade or go underground. The desert cools quickly when the sun is low in the sky, so they come out in the evening, at night, or in early morning. A few can stay active even in the hottest periods of the day. Rodents are the most successful desert mammals of all— the greatest in number and in number of different species.

Though the desert air is hot and dry, an underground burrow will be 60° or 70° F. and moist. The GRASSHOPPER MOUSE stays below until night and then comes out to hunt for insects, scorpions, lizards, and mice. The juicy prey supply enough water so the animal does not need to drink.

The ANTELOPE GROUND SQUIRREL is named for the pronghorn antelope; like the pronghorn, it has a white rump. It is one of the few small mammals of the desert that feed above ground in daytime even in the heat of summer. It gets water by adding insects to its plant diet and can go for months without drinking. This animal shows no distress even when its body temperature rises to a fever level of 110° F. or more. When it does get too hot, it scurries into the burrow and sprawls against the cool ground to lower its temperature. Sometimes it wets its chest fur with saliva to cool its body by evaporation.

Some desert rodents go into a deep sleep called estivation (ess-tuh-VAY-shun) in the hottest part of the year. It is like hibernation in winter: The body temperature falls and breathing becomes slow. Some mice enter this state each day during the hottest hours and then wake in the evening. But the MOJAVE (muh-HAHV-ee) GROUND SQUIRREL of California goes underground in early August and estivates until the end of February—seven months without eating or drinking!

Unlike desert mammals, almost all birds are active in daytime and few use burrows in the ground to escape the heat. Most birds seek shade when the sun is high in the sky, and the air above the ground—where birds live—is cooler than it is near the surface. Feathers are insulation; in summer they keep hot air away from the skin, just as they keep the cold out in winter. Birds have one other advantage for life in a hot climate: The normal body temperature of all birds is high—104° to 108° F. Usually the air is hotter than this for only a few hours in the middle of each day. When the heat is too great, birds have two ways of cooling off. Some birds pant, breathing with open mouths the way dogs do. Some cool themselves by flapping the loose skin that hangs under their throats. In both cases, the bird's temperature falls because of evaporation as its body loses water into the air. Like all animals, birds need water sources to replace the moisture they lose.

The male HOUSE FINCH has bright red on its head and chest; the female is a dull brown. These birds don't always live near houses, but in the desert they almost always live within two miles of drinking water. Their main food in all seasons is seeds, and with this dry diet the finches need to drink at least once each day.

The ASH-THROATED FLYCATCHER feeds on insects caught in the air. Birds that eat insects as their main food usually get enough moisture from their prey and can live without drinking water.

The BLACK-THROATED SPARROW changes its eating and drinking habits with the season. As long as there are plenty of insects, it gets enough water from these. When insects are scarce, this sparrow eats seeds, lives near a water hole, and drinks every day.

BURROWING OWLS live like desert rodents—in underground tunnels. They take over the burrow of some other animal or else they dig their own. Unlike other owls, they are often out in daylight, standing near the burrow entrance. In the evening and through the night, they hunt insects and rodents.

All the animals face the twin problems of little water and intense heat. Snakes and most desert lizards get enough water for their needs from their animal prey. Some reptiles drink the dew that forms on plants at night and from occasional rain puddles. Most reptiles retreat into estivation when conditions become too hot and dry, but as long as they stay active, they move in response to the daily shifts in temperature. Through the day they go into the sun or out of it, into shade or underground, to keep from becoming too hot or too cold. Most lizards are active in the daytime. Desert snakes are less tolerant of high temperatures, so they usually hunt at night.

The FRINGE-TOED LIZARD lives only in sandy areas. Though the lizard sometimes pants to cool off, it normally controls its temperature by avoiding too much heat. On hot days, it dashes from shade to shade. It crosses the sand on two legs to keep its body away from the burning surface. To escape the sun or danger, it dives into the sand and "swims" down out of sight. The "fringes" are scales on the back feet that make it easier to run on sand and help the lizard to push its body underground. It can remain buried for a long time, breathing the air between sand grains.

In hot weather, the fast-moving ZEBRA-TAILED LIZARD hunts insects early and late in the day. It, too, runs on its rear legs when moving at top speed (eighteen miles an hour). Like many lizards, its tail breaks off when an enemy pounces on it. The lizard escapes, and a new tail will grow back in.

The SIDEWINDER is a small rattlesnake and a nighttime hunter. In the day it may rest in a shallow hole in the shade until the heat drives it underground. A sidewinder moves by twisting its body into loops and throwing itself forward in a sideways direction.

Spadefoot toads may spend ten months or more of each year buried deep in the ground. When it rains any time during the warm months, they wake and rush to pools of water to find mates. Since the water may dry up in a few days or weeks, these amphibians survive on the desert only because their young develop so quickly. Eggs of COUCH'S SPADEFOOT may hatch in less than a day, and tadpoles change to tiny toads in as little as eight days.

sidewinder tracks in the sand

back foot of fringe-toed lizard (much enlarged)

Deserts contain a rich variety of arthropods. Although some of them have bodies with special adaptations for living in dry places, most do not. But insect bodies have one built-in feature that makes it easier to survive in deserts. Most adults have a thin, waxy covering just below the surface that prevents water loss into the air. In dry periods, most can meet their small water needs from their food or from dew, and some can absorb water from the air or soil. All protect themselves from water loss and heat by avoiding the sun at its hottest. In times of extreme dryness, many stop all activity. Like some mammals, they enter a summer resting state and their body processes slow down. They can remain quiet for days, weeks, or longer without needing food or drink.

The DESERT COCKROACH lives underground in sandy soil. Its smooth body slips through sand, and its legs are covered with stiff spines to push it along. At night it "swims" near the surface, feeding underground on the remains of dead plants and animals. To avoid the heat of day, it moves down a foot or more into the earth where the soil is cool and holds some moisture. It can absorb water through its body from the damp sand.

An ANT LION is the larva of a lacewing insect. The ant lion digs a pit and waits near the bottom. When an insect stumbles into the pit, the ant lion snaps it up. Pits are usually made in the shade. During the hot part of the day, the ant lion moves deeper into the ground.

TARANTULA HAWKS are large wasps that hunt tarantulas to feed their young. When a female wasp is ready to lay an egg, she finds a tarantula in its burrow and stings it, leaving the spider paralyzed. She drags the victim to a hole she has made in the ground, lays her egg or eggs upon the tarantula, and buries it. When the wasp larva hatches, it will find a live food supply.

These LAND SNAILS become inactive in hot, dry weather. Soft body parts slip back into the protective shell. The snails produce mucus at the open end of their shells and glue themselves to the surface of plants. Their bodies slow. Even in full sun, in this state the snails lose very little water into the dry air.

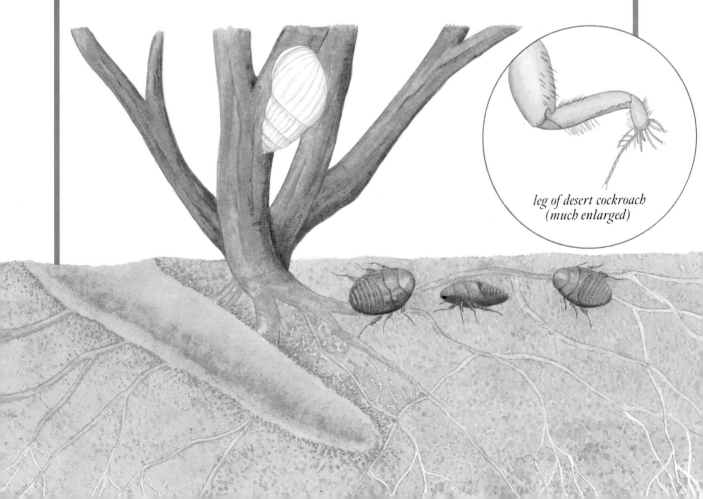

leg of desert cockroach
(much enlarged)

Most of the plants we see have green leaves that make food to fuel the plant's life and growth. In the presence of sunshine, green chlorophyll in the leaves uses water from the soil and gas from the air to make the food, in the form of sugar. During the day, gases move in and out of leaves through tiny openings on the leaf surface. Some of the moisture inside the plant also passes out through the tiny openings and evaporates into the dry desert air. When the soil is dry and no water is coming in from the roots, the plant loses more water than it can replace. Without moisture, it wilts and may die. Desert perennials have developed different ways of storing and conserving water.

Like PERRY'S AGAVE (ah-GAH-vee), many desert plants have thick, juicy leaves filled with large cells that store water. Agave leaves are stiff and sharply pointed, and they grow close to the ground in a thick, round cluster. The outer layer of the leaves is thick and contains a waxy waterproofing material. The leaves have fewer pores than ordinary leaves and "breathe" at night instead of in the day. Agaves are called century plants because they are said to flower only once in one hundred years. In fact, most live eight to twenty years before a tall flower stalk grows up from the low clump of leaves. After flowering and making its seeds, the whole plant dies.

Most cacti are leafless and have thick stems. These juicy stems are similar to the leaves on plants such as agave. They have thick, waxy skins, fewer breathing holes, and large water-holding cells; they open their pores at night. The stems contain chlorophyll and take over the job of making food that is usually done by plant leaves. This prickly cactus, called the JUMPING CHOLLA (CHOY-yuh) sometimes grows as a small tree. It doesn't really jump, but its joints break off at the slightest touch.

OCOTILLO (oh-kuh-TEE-yoh) has straight branches growing twelve feet long or more. The woody stems are bare much of the year. After rainfall in any season, a new set of leaves grows on the branches. They drop off when the land dries again, and the green stems take over the work of making food for the plant. Ocotillo may have five or six crops of leaves in a year. It bears red flowers in spring and may blossom again in any month in which there is rain.

The small leaves of FOOTHILL PALO VERDE (PA-loh VUR-dee) trees appear in spring and drop off in the dry season. *Palo verde* means "green stick." The bark is green in color and contains chlorophyll. When the palo verde stands leafless, the bare branches make all the food for the tree.

flowers of
Perry's agave

ocotillo flowers

FALL—MAMMALS

Now the growing season for most plants is ending, and the plants are hung with ripe fruits. Seed-eating animals are gathering food for winter, and some mammals are preparing for hibernation. Many bats—the flying mammals—will escape from winter entirely by traveling southward. Deer, peccaries, rabbits, and the large hunting mammals—animals without burrows and without stored food—face a more difficult life in the season ahead.

PACK RATS stay active all year, but they prepare for winter by storing seeds and fruits. They pile up sticks, leaves, and stones on top of their nests and put clusters of prickly cactus at the entrance to keep other animals away. Pack rats are famous for their nightly collecting habits. They have been known to carry off a camper's socks—even false teeth!—and bring them to the den.

The KANGAROO RAT has large rear legs and small front ones and moves by jumping. In fall it may collect several bushels of seeds for underground storage. It can live its whole life on a dry diet of seeds. It doesn't need drinking water or the moisture in juicy plants. Like other rodents, it has few sweat glands, so it doesn't lose much moisture by sweating. It stays in a cool burrow during the daytime heat, and only a small amount of water passes out of its system with its body wastes. Even dry seeds contain a little moisture, so it gets a bit of water from the seeds and a bit more from the tiny amount that is produced in the body as an animal turns its food into energy. This is less than other animals need but enough for the kangaroo rat.

Flocks of MEXICAN FREE-TAILED BATS live in the desert during the warm months, feeding on small moths. Most of these bats fly back to Mexico in the fall. Some stay in the United States and hibernate in caves or empty buildings. The hibernators put on extra fat by feeding heavily in the fall and live off this fat over the winter.

Desert COYOTES are like other coyotes but smaller and with lighter-colored fur. Coyotes hunt in all seasons of the year. They dig up ground squirrels, mice, and rats from burrows, and they chase down jackrabbits and cottontails.

FALL—BIRDS

Adult birds are worn and thin after the work of raising their young, and their feathers are torn and faded from hard use. Birds that live among cacti and thorny bushes suffer even more wear and tear than do birds in other habitats. In late summer and fall, their worn feathers fall out as new ones grow in. The new feathers on many of the brightly colored birds are duller than those worn in the mating season. Fall is a time of eager feeding. The birds need energy to grow their new feathers, and migrators are storing fat that will give them fuel for the journey. From late August through September, the fall migration is in full swing. Winter visitors, coming to spend the cold months in the desert, begin to arrive in October.

LUCY'S WARBLER is the only member of the warbler family that nests in these deserts. After the young are raised, these small gray birds leave to spend the winter in Mexico.

MOUNTAIN BLUEBIRDS nest in the western mountains of the United States and Canada and come down to warmer areas for the winter. In fall the male is covered by gray-tipped body feathers instead of the sky-blue feathers of spring. Bluebirds catch insects in flight or on the ground. Even in winter they eat very little plant food.

The LAZULI (la-ZOO-lee) BUNTING passes through the warm deserts in spring and fall, moving between its winter home in Mexico and its summer range farther north. This little bird has a thick bill for cracking hard seeds. Travel over the dry desert is dangerous for migrating seed eaters. Temperatures are still high for many hours of the day. The bunting will not survive unless it finds water along the way.

The LOGGERHEAD SHRIKE stays in the desert all year. This hunter eats insects, lizards, small rodents, and an occasional bird. Shrikes are known as butcher birds because they hang their dead prey on a thorn or cactus needle. Unlike hawks, shrikes do not have strong claws for holding prey. With the victim pinned in place, they can tear the food apart and eat it more easily.

Most reptiles hibernate for at least part of the winter, even in warm desert areas. In the fall, some travel to special winter dens, while others find convenient holes that were made by mammals and hibernate there. Still others will not hibernate until December or January, and some small-bodied animals will remain active even in the coldest months. For them, the only change in fall is to shift their activities toward the warmer daylight hours.

GOPHER SNAKES are large animals (up to seven feet long) with dark markings along their bodies. Sometimes the marks are diamond-shaped. Because of this, and because they flatten their heads when they are threatened, they are sometimes mistaken for rattlesnakes. In late fall, gopher snakes hibernate in rock crevices or animal burrows.

Unlike other desert lizards, the big, harmless CHUCKWALLA is a vegetarian. It eats flowers, fruits, and leaves. Starting in late summer, this animal spends less and less time above ground. In very dry years and in areas with no summer rain, the chuckwalla disappears from sight from mid-August until spring. It lives among rocks and takes shelter by crawling into deep cracks. If it is disturbed there, the lizard gulps in air and swells up like a balloon. Wedged firmly in the crack, the chuckwalla can't be pulled out.

Geckos are unusual among lizards because most of them are active at night rather than by day, searching for insects and spiders. When they eat more food than they need, they store the extra fat in their tails. The BANDED GECKO retreats underground in October and remains inactive until March. In this resting state, it could live on its stored fat for up to nine months.

The YUCCA (YUCK-uh) NIGHT LIZARD is typically found in or around yucca plants. This little lizard crawls through the yuccas hunting for insects and spiders, hides among the branches, and rests under the fallen plant litter. In the warmer desert areas, it is active and feeding all through the year.

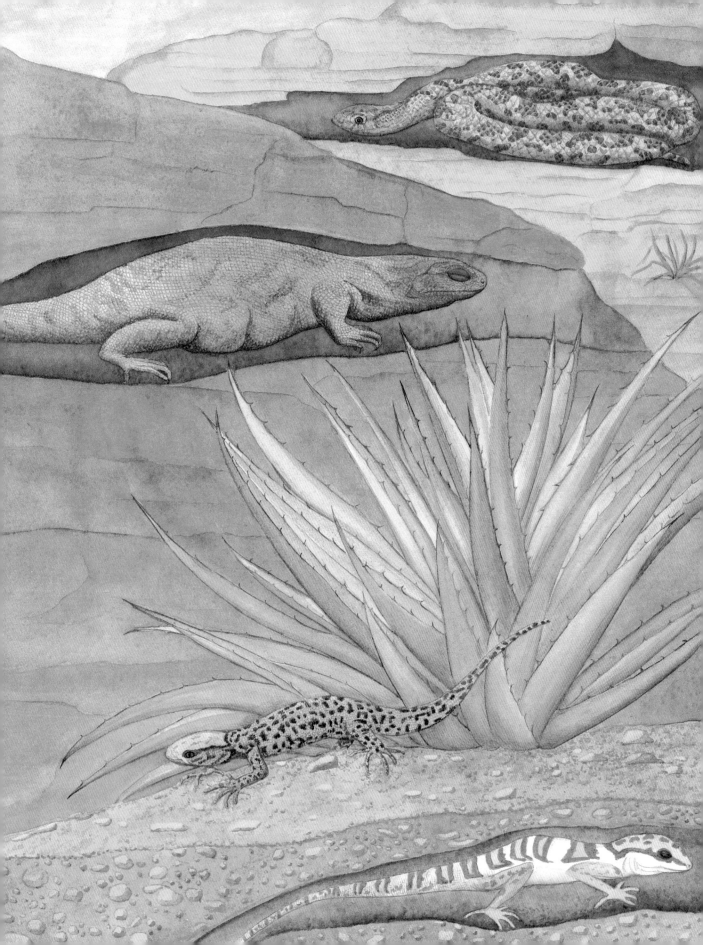

FALL—ARTHROPODS

A great many arthropods feed on waste plant and animal matter, and these animals play an important role as decomposers. They break down these materials, returning to the soil the chemicals that are bound up in the dead tissues. But arthropods can be active only when the weather is favorable—when it is neither too cold, too hot, nor too dry. Now, as the fall nights become cooler, many of them are disappearing from sight.

Most TERMITES in hot deserts have underground nests. They move quantities of dead plants down to the nests of the colony. This species eats plants, digests them, and then uses its own droppings as the material for building long tubes attached to the stems of plants. The droppings are rich in nitrogen and other chemicals needed for plant growth. When it rains again, the water will wash the material down to the ground and fertilize the desert.

DUNG BEETLES collect the droppings of mammals, shape them into balls, and

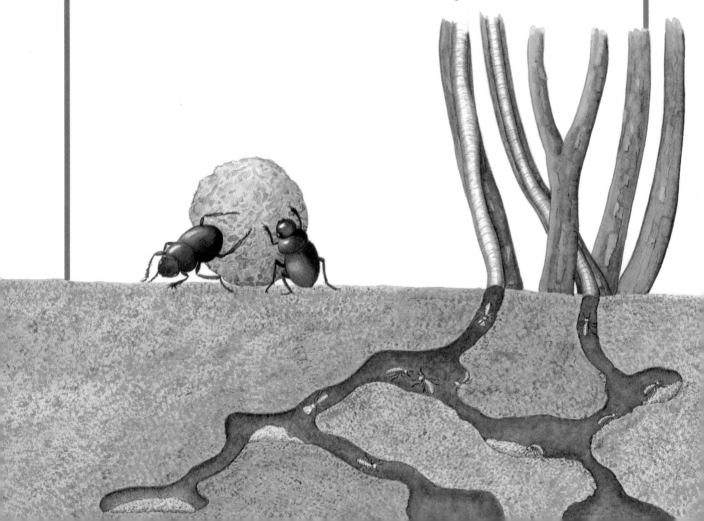

bury them in the ground. They use this animal waste as food, but they often collect more than they actually eat. The waste breaks down more quickly underground than it would lying on the dry earth, and the buried droppings soon add their richness to the soil.

Unlike insects, MILLIPEDES (MILL-uh-peeds), or "thousand leggers," have no waxy outer layer to prevent them from losing body water, but this species manages to live in many desert areas. Like other desert animals, the millipede avoids intense heat by moving into shade or an underground burrow. It feeds on dead plants, but only during three or four months of the year. In the fall, it burrows into the ground and goes into a resting state that will last until rain falls next summer. During these months, it eats nothing but takes in water from the soil through its skin.

Cocoons of YUCCA (YUCK-uh) MOTHS are also in the ground, a few inches deep. Last spring a female moth pollinated a yucca flower while leaving her eggs there. As the flower developed into a fruit, the larvae that hatched from the eggs fed on some of the seeds in the growing pod. This is the only food that the yucca moth larvae can eat. In fall the larvae dropped to the ground, dug down into the soil, and changed to pupae. Next spring, when the yucca blooms again, the adult moths will come out of their cocoons and mate. Then once again the female moths will fertilize the yuccas as the eggs are laid.

yucca moth on flower

A new crop of wildflowers blooms late in the growing season, touching the desert with a final splash of color. Many trees and bushes have bare branches now, but some of the commonest ones will keep their leaves all through the fall and winter months. Ripening fruits on plants of all kinds signal that the growing year is ending, and the animals are harvesting these fruits and the nourishing seeds they contain. Whatever the animals leave becomes a part of the great seed bank, waiting in the earth for some future desert year.

Some CHINCHWEED plants are still blooming in early fall. This plant is one of the summer annuals—wildflowers whose seeds sprout only if they receive the right combination of rainfall and hot weather. If the summer and fall rains are poor, the seeds remain in the soil for another year.

Depending upon conditions, MESQUITE (meh-SKEET) may grow as a shrub or a tree. Its branches are bare of leaves in the fall but hung with fruits. These long pods are sweet-tasting, and each holds fifty to sixty seeds. Though many mammals and birds eat the pods, the seeds have a hard coat and usually pass through their bodies without being digested.

CREOSOTE (KREE-uh-soht) BUSH is the most common shrub in North American deserts. The name refers to its smell. When the leaves are wet with rain, they have a strong tarlike odor. The plant is an evergreen, but in dry periods the leaves fall off and a crop of very small ones takes over the work of making food for the plant. Even when they dry out and lose half of their moisture, these new leaves are able to do the job.

DESERT MISTLETOE grows on mesquite, palo verde, and other trees belonging to the pea family. Mistletoe has no leaves, but its stems contain chlorophyll and manufacture some food. Its roots grow into the supporting branches and draw nourishment from the host tree. Mistletoe has fruits from November until spring. The berries are an important food for the phainopepla (fay-nuh-PEP-luh) and other birds. Bird droppings containing the mistletoe seeds fall on the tree branches and "plant" a new crop of mistletoe.

mistletoe
with fruits

spring flowers of
creosote bush

GLOSSARY

Amphibian. The word means "double-living": Amphibian animals begin life in wet places and later move to the land. They are born from eggs without shells. Like reptiles, they depend on outside sources for most of their body heat.

Annual. A plant that completes its life cycle in a year or less. See pages 14 and 24.

Arthropod. An animal whose body is made up of segments and enclosed in an outside skeleton. Arthropods include insects, lobsters, and spiders.

Chlorophyll. The green matter in plants that uses the sun's energy to turn raw materials into food. See page 34.

Ephemeral. Lasting a very short time. See page 24.

Estivation. A resting condition that is similar to hibernation but occurs in the summer. See page 26.

Hibernation. A condition of rest and quiet in winter, in which activity stops and the body processes slow down sharply. See page 6.

Larva (plural: *larvae*). A stage in the life of some insects, coming after they hatch from the egg and before they change to pupae.

Perennial. A plant that lives year after year. See pages 14 and 24.

Pupa (plural: *pupae*). A resting period in the life of some insects, coming between the larval and the adult stages. As a pupa, some insects are enclosed in a covering, such as a cocoon.

Reptile. Most reptiles hatch from shelled eggs, but some are born alive. They have scales on their skins and claws on their toes. Like amphibians, they need outside sources of heat to keep their bodies warm.

BOOKS ABOUT DESERT LIFE

Cornett, James W. *Wildlife of North American Deserts*. Palm Springs, Calif.: Nature Trails Press, 1987.

Dodge, Natt N. *Flowers of the Southwest Deserts*. Tucson, Ariz.: Southwest Parks and Monument Association, 1985.

Larson, Peggy. *The Sierra Club Naturalist's Guide to the Deserts of the Southwest*. San Francisco: Sierra Club Books, 1977.

MacMahon, James. *Deserts*. The Audubon Society Nature Guides. New York: Alfred A. Knopf, 1985.

Niehaus, Theodore F. *A Field Guide to Southwestern and Texas Wildflowers*. The Peterson Field Guide Series. New York: Houghton Mifflin, 1984.

Sutton, Ann, and Myron Sutton. *The Life of the Desert*. New York: McGraw-Hill, 1966.

INDEX

The scientific names are shown in *italics*.
The illustration pages appear in **boldface**.